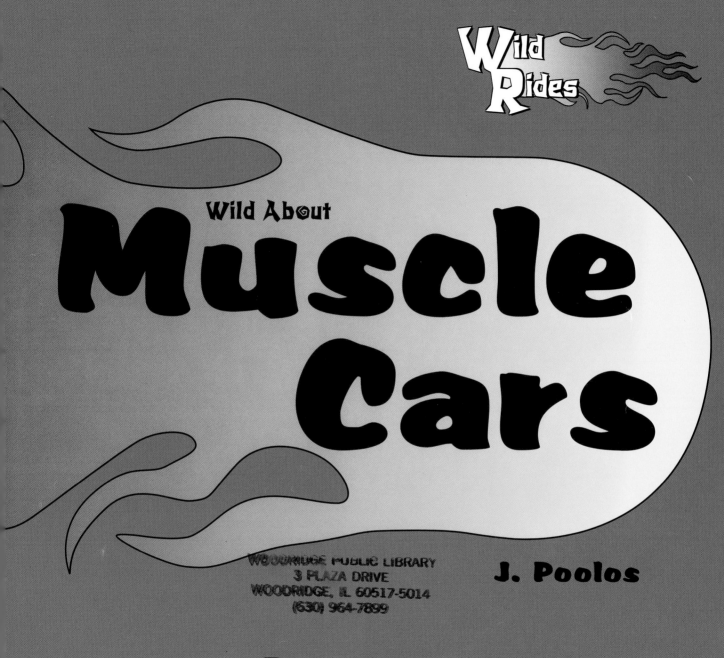

Wild Rides

Wild About

# Muscle Cars

J. Poolos

**PowerKiDS**
press.

New York

Published in 2008 by The Rosen Publishing Group, Inc.
29 East 21st Street, New York, NY 10010

First Edition

Editor: Amelie von Zumbusch
Book Design: Greg Tucker
Photo Researcher: Nicole Pristash

Photo Credits: Cover, pp. 5, 9, 11, 19, 21 © Shutterstock.com; p. 7 © R. Gates/Getty Images; pp. 13, 15, 17 © Ron Kimball/Ron Kimball Stock.

Cataloging-in-Publication Data

Poolos, Jamie.
   Wild about muscle cars / J. Poolos. — 1st ed.
      p. cm. — (Wild rides)
   Includes index.
   ISBN-13: 978-1-4042-3788-9 (library binding)
   ISBN-10: 1-4042-3788-7 (library binding)
   1. Muscle cars—Juvenile literature. 2. Automobiles—United States—Juvenile literature. I. Title.
   TL23.P59 2008
   629.222—dc22
                                          2006039583

Manufactured in the United States of America

# Contents

# Muscle Cars Rock!

A muscle car is a fast car with a strong **engine**. Muscle cars were made in the United States between the late 1950s and the early 1970s. In many ways, a muscle car is like many other midsize cars of that time. It has an engine, four wheels, a **steering** wheel, and seats.

However, a muscle car is built for speed! Its engine is powerful. Its wheels are **chrome**, and its tires are big and wide. A muscle car can race down a quarter-mile (.4 km) **drag strip** in about 5 seconds. That is fast!

This muscle car is drag racing at the Santa Pod Raceway, in Podington, Great Britain.

# The Muscle Car Age

During the 1950s, carmakers figured out that many American car buyers wanted faster cars. In 1957, the carmaker American Motors put a powerful engine into one of its family cars. They called it the Rambler Rebel, the fastest four-door car in America.

Over the years, muscle cars grew more **popular**. Young drivers liked muscle cars because the cars were powerful, looked cool, and were not expensive. However, in 1973, gas became much more expensive. People did not want cars with big engines that used a lot of gas. Carmakers stopped selling muscle cars.

This photo of a muscle car called the Ford GT Torino was taken during the 1960s. Muscle cars were popular throughout the 1960s.

# Cool-Looking Cars

Muscle cars look much like everyday family cars, but they have **details** that set them apart. Muscle cars have shiny paint, sometimes with a racing stripe on the **hood**. They have shiny, chrome wheels. They have thick, wide tires on the back wheels. These tires are called slicks.

Some muscle cars have spoilers on the **trunk**. A spoiler is like a big wing. As the car moves forward, the air moving over the spoiler helps hold the car to the road. Some muscle cars have hood scoops. Hood scoops feed air into the engine and make cars run faster.

The red and white striped object on the back of this Chevrolet Camaro's trunk is a spoiler.

# Muscle Car Engines

Muscle car engines are big and powerful. Engine size is measured in cubic inches. One cubic inch is like a box whose sides are each one inch (2.5 cm) long and wide. The first muscle car's engine was 327 cubic inches (5.4 L). Over time, muscle car engines grew even larger!

By the mid-1970s, muscle car engines were bigger and more powerful than ever. Engine power is measured in horsepower. Most muscle car engines made between 350 and 420 horsepower. The Ford 427 Cammer was the most powerful muscle car engine ever made. It made 657 horsepower.

Muscle car owners work hard to keep their cars' engines clean. Shiny engines look cool and help the car run well.

# The Pontiac GTO

The most famous muscle car is the Pontiac GTO, nicknamed the Goat. The GTO was **designed** by Russell Gee and John DeLorean. The first GTO rolled out of the factory in 1964 with an engine that made 360 horsepower. It reached 60 miles per hour (97 km/h) in 6.1 seconds and ran the quarter mile (.4 km) in 14.5 seconds at 102 miles per hour (164 km/h).

Later GTOs were even faster. The 1969 model reached 60 miles per hour (97 km/h) in 5.2 seconds and ran the quarter mile in 11.5 seconds at 123 miles per hour (198 km/h).

Some 1969 GTOs, like this car, were the Judge model. The Judge had a spoiler and wider tires than most GTOs.

# The Dodge Charger

With the Pontiac GTO ruling the streets, the carmaker Dodge decided to make its own muscle car. In 1966, it produced the Charger, one of the most famous muscle cars of all time. Carl Cameron designed the car. It was the first American car to have a spoiler. It had a 426-cubic-inch (7-L) Hemi engine that made between 450 and 475 horsepower.

Owners would soup up their cars, or make changes to them to make them go even faster. One famous Charger was the General Lee. The General Lee was driven by the stars of the television show *The Dukes of Hazzard*.

The owner of this 1968 Charger souped up the car by taking off its hood and adding a big, powerful engine.

# The 1968 Oldsmobile Cutlass 442

Some muscle cars were so fast that they were hard to drive around town. The Oldsmobile Cutlass 442 was both fast and easy to drive, though. Oldsmobile first made the car in 1964 using parts the company made for police cars.

Later the company decided to improve the car so it could **compete** with other muscle cars. The 1968 model had a 400-cubic-inch (6.6-L) engine that made 390 horsepower. It had a Hurst Dual-Gate shifter, which let drivers shift, or change **gears**, smoothly. It also had special one-person seats called bucket seats.

Some 1968 Oldsmobile Cutlass 442s had a hard top. Other 442s, like this one, had a soft top you could put down.

# Muscle Car Rallies and Drag Races

Muscle cars have come back into style today. They are popular among adults who owned them when they were young. Some people buy the old cars and **restore** them. They take their cars to old-car rallies, or gatherings. They show the cars off to other people who love muscle cars. Sometimes they have parades and **contests** for the best muscle car.

Other people race their muscle cars at drag strips. They tune their cars to make them go superfast. Race winners get **trophies** and sometimes even win money.

These muscle cars are lined up at a car show so that car fans can get a good look at them.

# Modern Muscle Cars

Muscle cars became so popular that carmakers started to make brand-new muscle cars. These cars are called modern muscle cars. Some modern muscle cars share the names of old muscle cars. The Dodge Charger and the Pontiac GTO are two such cars. These cars use modern **technology**. They are more comfortable than old muscle cars. They are easier to drive and break down less often.

Modern muscle cars have the same cool look that yesterday's muscle cars had. They have shiny paint, thick tires, and even hood scoops. Most importantly, they have big, powerful engines.

This modern muscle car is the Chevrolet Corvette Z06. It can go as fast as 171 miles per hour (275 km/h).

# Muscle Cars Forever!

People love muscle cars. They are fun to collect, fix up, show, and race. They remind us of a time when ordinary people could buy cars that were big and fast. In fact, carmakers may never build inexpensive cars that are as fast or as powerful as the old muscle cars again.

As muscle car fans bring back more of the old cars and make them look like new, there will be more and more muscle cars on the road. Perhaps someone you know drives a muscle car. Maybe someday you will even drive one of your own.

# Glossary

**chrome** (KROHM)  A shiny metal that is used on cars and motorcycles.

**compete** (kum-PEET)  To go against another in a game or test.

**contests** (KAN-tests)  Games in which two or more people try to win a prize.

**designed** (dih-ZYND)  Planned the form of something.

**details** (DEE-taylz)  The small parts of something.

**drag strip** (DRAG STRIP)  A place where two cars or motorcycles race each other.

**engine** (EN-jin)  A machine inside a car or airplane that makes the car or airplane move.

**gears** (GEERZ)  Parts of a machine that help it work.

**hood** (HUD)  The cover over a car's engine.

**popular** (PAH-pyuh-lur)  Liked by lots of people.

**restore** (rih-STOR)  To put back, to return to an earlier state.

**steering** (STEER-ing)  Having to do with guiding something's path.

**technology** (tek-NAH-luh-jee)  The science of everyday life.

**trophies** (TROH-feez)  Prizes that are often shaped like a cup.

**trunk** (TRUNK)  The covered part in the back of a car.

# Index

# Web Sites

Due to the changing nature of Internet links, PowerKids Press has developed an online list of Web sites related to the subject of this book. This site is updated regularly. Please use this link to access the list: www.powerkidslinks.com/wild/muscle/